Middle School Note Taking and Outlining

Table of Contents

Introduction ~~~~~~2

Pretest ~~~~~~3

Unit 1: Reference Resources
Choosing Reference Resources ~~~~~~~~~~~~~~~~~~~~~~~~~5
Kinds of Books ~~~~~~~~~~~~~~~~~~~~~~~~~~~~~~~~~~6
Navigating the Library ~~~~~~~~~~~~~~~~~~~~~~~~~~~~~7
The Reader's Guide ~~~~~~~~~~~~~~~~~~~~~~~~~~~~~~8
The Internet as a Reference Resource ~~~~~~~~~~~~~~~~~~~~9
Narrowing the Search ~~~~~~~~~~~~~~~~~~~~~~~~~~~~~11
Online Reference Resources ~~~~~~~~~~~~~~~~~~~~~~~~~~12

Unit 2: Note Taking
Brainstorming ~~~~~~~~~~~~~~~~~~~~~~~~~~~~~~~~~13
Fact and Opinion ~~~~~~~~~~~~~~~~~~~~~~~~~~~~~~~~14
Note Taking ~~~~~~~~~~~~~~~~~~~~~~~~~~~~~~~~~~~15
Topic and Audience ~~~~~~~~~~~~~~~~~~~~~~~~~~~~~~17
Notes Based on an Interview ~~~~~~~~~~~~~~~~~~~~~~~~19
Organizing and Taking Notes ~~~~~~~~~~~~~~~~~~~~~~~~20
Summarizing ~~~~~~~~~~~~~~~~~~~~~~~~~~~~~~~~~~21
Paraphrasing ~~~~~~~~~~~~~~~~~~~~~~~~~~~~~~~~~~23
Direct Quotations ~~~~~~~~~~~~~~~~~~~~~~~~~~~~~~~25
Selecting Essential Information ~~~~~~~~~~~~~~~~~~~~~~~27
Using Examples ~~~~~~~~~~~~~~~~~~~~~~~~~~~~~~~~28
Practice, Practice, Practice ~~~~~~~~~~~~~~~~~~~~~~~~~29

Unit 3: Outlining
Introduction to Outlines ~~~~~~~~~~~~~~~~~~~~~~~~~~~32
Outlining a Plan ~~~~~~~~~~~~~~~~~~~~~~~~~~~~~~~33
Outlining ~~~~~~~~~~~~~~~~~~~~~~~~~~~~~~~~~~~~35
Thesis Statements and Outlines ~~~~~~~~~~~~~~~~~~~~~~37
Supporting Details and Outlines ~~~~~~~~~~~~~~~~~~~~~~38

Unit 4: Footnotes and Bibliographies
Footnotes and Appendix ~~~~~~~~~~~~~~~~~~~~~~~~~~~39
Documenting Your Sources ~~~~~~~~~~~~~~~~~~~~~~~~~41
Writing a Bibliography ~~~~~~~~~~~~~~~~~~~~~~~~~~~43
Practice, Practice ~~~~~~~~~~~~~~~~~~~~~~~~~~~~~~45

Posttest ~~~~~~~~~~~~~~~~~~~~~~~~~~~~~~~~~~~~~47

Answer Key ~~~~~~~~~~~~~~~~~~~~~~~~~~~~~~~~~~49

D1385301

Introduction

This book is designed to review and reinforce the research and reference skills and the writing skills that students will need in middle school. The standards of the National Council of Teachers of English (NCTE) state that students should conduct research on issues and interests by generating ideas and questions, and by posing problems. They should gather, evaluate, and synthesize data from a variety of sources (e.g., print and nonprint texts, artifacts, people) to communicate their discoveries in ways that suit their purpose and audience. Students should use a variety of technological and information resources (e.g., libraries, databases, computer networks, video) to gather and synthesize information and to create and communicate knowledge. Students should adjust their use of spoken, written, and visual language (e.g., conventions, style, vocabulary) to communicate effectively with a variety of audiences and for different purposes. Students should employ a wide range of strategies as they write and use different writing processes appropriately to communicate with different audiences for a variety of purposes. *Middle School Note Taking and Outlining* is designed for students who may require additional practice in the basics of identifying and locating reference materials and using these materials to prepare written reports. It can be used effectively as a tool to reinforce skills at school or at home.

Organization

These activities are designed for middle school students who will be using reference materials to take notes and to create outlines for research reports. This book is divided into four units: Reference Resources, Note Taking, Outlining, and Footnotes and Bibliographies. Assessment tests at the beginning and end of the book will help teachers or parents to evaluate the students' understanding of the subjects and to show areas where more practice may be needed.

Use

This book has been designed for independent or group use by students who have been introduced to the skills and concepts described. Copies of the activities can be given to individuals, pairs of students, or small groups for completion. They may be used as a center activity. If students are familiar with the content, the worksheets may also be used as homework. Each lesson is introduced with a model at the top of the page and ends with a meaningful, reinforcing exercise at the bottom of the page. Each lesson is clearly labeled, and directions are clear and uncomplicated. Most students can use *Middle School Note Taking and Outlining* with a high degree of independence.

Additional Notes

1. Student Communication: Be sure to discuss with your students what they will be doing and what it means. Assure the students that these worksheets are for practice purposes to help them improve their research, reference, and writing skills.

2. The Internet: The section in Unit 1 that focuses on the Internet as a reference tool for students is carefully designed to make sure that students use specific search engines in the exercises. This will ensure that students will not encounter any unsuitable materials.

3. Make It Fun: Research and writing can be enjoyable! Make the work fun and meaningful when possible. For example, after a discussion and work with notes and note taking, find a way to relate the information to the students' own lives. If your class is doing a school project or there is a national event or famous person that has caught the interest of the class, focus the students on researching related topics. The results should be fun for everyone!

Name _____   Date _____

Pretest

Tell which reference source you would use to find the following information. Circle (A) for encyclopedia, (B) for thesaurus, (C) for Reader's Guide, or (D) for atlas.

1. An antonym for the word *clever*
    A.   **B.**   **C.**   **D.**

2. Information on Quebec, Canada
    A.   **B.**   **C.**   **D.**

3. The location of the Saginaw River
    A.   **B.**   **C.**   **D.**

4. A recent article on toxic waste
    A.   **B.**   **C.**   **D.**

5. The life of Alexander the Great
    A.   **B.**   **C.**   **D.**

6. An article written by George Maliff
    A.   **B.**   **C.**   **D.**

7. A synonym for the word *lovely*
    A.   **B.**   **C.**   **D.**

Circle the correct answer for each question.

8. Which reference source does *not* use guide words?
    A. dictionary   **B.** atlas   **C.** encyclopedia

9. Which would you *not* use a dictionary to find?
    A. word origin   **B.** magazine articles   **C.** syllables

10. Which would you *not* find in a book?
    A. copyright page   **B.** table of contents   **C.** *Reader's Guide*

Circle the letter by the answer that best completes the sentence.

11. It is important to write the name of the book and the _____ when writing notes on a note card.
    A. author   **B.** table of contents   **C.** glossary   **D.** chapter

12. A good writer uses a different _____ for each new question.
    A. note card   **B.** table of contents   **C.** glossary   **D.** chapter

13. The _____ is what a paragraph or story is mostly about.
    A. detail   **B.** fact   **C.** conclusion   **D.** main idea

14. An opinion is based on what someone _____.
    A. says   **B.** thinks   **C.** reads   **D.** proves

Go on to the next page.

Pretest, p. 2

DIRECTIONS

Using the example outline triangle, fill in the missing lines in the partially completed outline triangles.

Example:

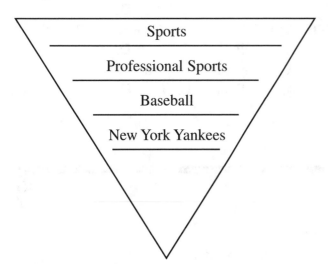

Sports

Professional Sports

Baseball

New York Yankees

15.

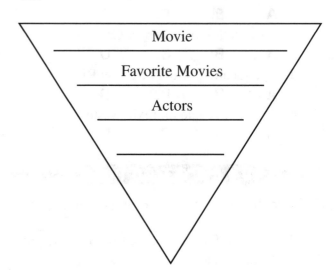

Movie

Favorite Movies

Actors

_____

16.

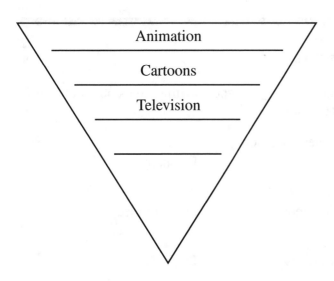

Animation

Cartoons

Television

_____

17.

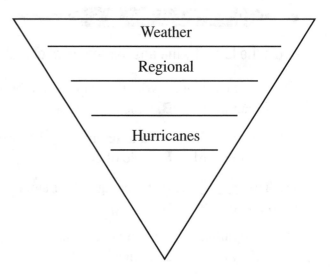

Weather

Regional

_____

Hurricanes

Name _____ Date _____

Choosing Reference Resources

When you are looking for reference materials, the **library** is an excellent place to find resources. Use the **Internet** as an alternative or supplement to the publications listed. You may also have some of the reference sources at home.

Use a **dictionary** to find the definitions and pronunciations of words, suggestions for word usage, and etymologies.

Use an **encyclopedia** to find articles about people, places, and other subjects. Use an encyclopedia to find references to related subjects.

Use a **thesaurus** to find synonyms and antonyms.

Use the ***Reader's Guide to Periodical Literature*** to find magazine articles on specific subjects or by particular authors.

Use an **atlas** to find maps and other information about geographical locations.

Use an **almanac**, an annual publication, to find such information as population numbers, annual rainfall, election statistics, and other specific information for a given year.

DIRECTIONS

Write *dictionary, encyclopedia, thesaurus, Reader's Guide, atlas,* or *almanac* to show where you would find the following information. Some information may be found in more than one source.

_____ **1.** The life of Queen Elizabeth I

_____ **2.** An article on the latest space shuttle flight

_____ **3.** The states and provinces through which the Rocky Mountains run

_____ **4.** The origin of the word *tomato*

_____ **5.** The annual rainfall for Somalia

_____ **6.** The most direct route from California to Alberta

_____ **7.** An antonym for the word *happy*

_____ **8.** The meaning of the word *spar*

_____ **9.** Recent articles on the subject of air pollution

_____ **10.** The pronunciation of the word *wren*

_____ **11.** The life of Sigmund Freud

_____ **12.** A synonym for the word *bad*

_____ **13.** The years during which World War I was fought

_____ **14.** An article on rock climbing

_____ **15.** The final standings of the National Hockey League for last year

Kinds of Books

The library has different kinds of books. Often, each kind of reading material is found in a separate section or room of a library.

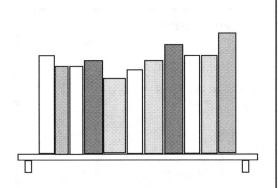

Fiction books include novels and short stories.
Nonfiction books tell facts about real people, places, things, or events.
A **biography** is a nonfiction book that tells about the life of a real person.
Reference books, such as encyclopedias, atlases, and dictionaries, are good sources of information on many subjects.
A **periodical** is a published work that appears in a series. Newspapers and magazines are periodicals.

DIRECTIONS

Name the section of the library in which you would find each of the following. Write *fiction, nonfiction, biography, reference,* or *periodical.*

_____ **1.** A book called *Scary Stories from Around the Campfire*

_____ **2.** A book about the history of the National Park Service

_____ **3.** A magazine from the American Camping Association

_____ **4.** The years Richard F. Pease was on the National Board of Directors for the American Camping Association

_____ **5.** Maps of camping areas in your state

_____ **6.** A book called *How to Set Up a Campsite*

_____ **7.** A book that tells about the life of Juliette Low

_____ **8.** A newspaper article about summer camps

_____ **9.** An article in *Time* about the popularity of day camps

_____ **10.** The etymology of the word *camp*

Name _____   Date _____

Navigating the Library

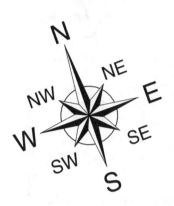

Books are arranged on library shelves according to the **Dewey Decimal System**. Each book is assigned a number from 000 to 999, according to its subject matter. There are ten main subject areas. The following are the main subject areas for call numbers.

000–099   Reference (encyclopedias, atlases, newspapers)
100–199   Philosophy (ideas about the meaning of life, psychology)
200–299   Religion (world religion, mythology)
300–399   Social Sciences (government, law, business, education)
400–499   Languages (dictionaries, grammar books)
500–599   Pure Science (mathematics, chemistry, plants, animals)
600–699   Applied Science (how-to books, engineering, radio)
700–799   Arts and Recreation (music, art, sports, hobbies)
800–899   Literature (poems, plays, essays)
900–999   History and Geography (travel, biography)

DIRECTIONS

Write the call number group in which you would find each book.

1. *World Almanac and Book of Facts*

_____

2. *Mathematics for Today*

_____

3. *Philosophy Through the Ages*

_____

4. *Spanish: A Romance Language*

_____

5. *Technology Takes Over*

_____

6. *Splitting the Atom*

_____

7. *The Impressionist School of Painting*

_____

8. *Myths from Around the World*

_____

9. *The Study of Forgotten Societies*

_____

10. *The New Russia*

_____

11. *The Religions of the World*

_____

12. *The Reader's Guide*

_____

DIRECTIONS

Write the titles of three of your favorite books. Write the call number range beside each title.

13. _____

14. _____

15. _____

www.svschoolsupply.com
© Steck-Vaughn Company

Unit 1: Reference Resources
MS Note Taking and Outlining, SV 2926-2

The Reader's Guide

In libraries today, the *Reader's Guide to Periodical Literature* is available as a reference resource in two versions. The older version is a multivolume set of books. The newer version is on the library computer database at some libraries. One example of the new version is called *InfoTrac*. The computerized version resembles to some degree the older written version. At many libraries, if you need references written before the year 1980, you may have to use the older written version.

The **Reader's Guide to Periodical Literature** lists by author and by subject all the articles that appear in nearly 200 magazines. Use the *Reader's Guide* when you need:
1. recent articles on a particular subject;
2. several articles written over a period of time about the same subject;
3. many articles written by the same author.

Subject Entry

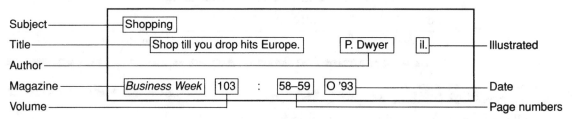

Author Entry

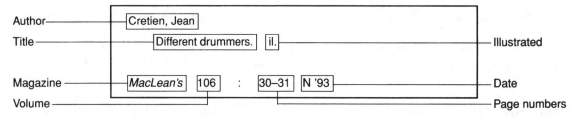

DIRECTIONS

Use the examples above to answer the questions.

1. Who wrote the article "Shop Till You Drop Hits Europe"? _____

2. Who is the author of "Different Drummers"? _____

3. In what magazine will you find the article "Shop Till You Drop Hits Europe"?

_____

4. Under what subject entry can you find the article "Shop Till You Drop Hits Europe"?

_____

5. In what volume of *MacLean's* does "Different Drummers" appear? _____

6. In what month and year was "Different Drummers" published? _____

7. Which article is illustrated? _____

8. On what pages will you find the article "Shop Till You Drop Hits Europe"? _____

Name _____   Date _____

The Internet as a Reference Resource

One of the most fascinating resources available to students today is the **Internet**. More specifically for research, the **World Wide Web** will be introduced. Online searches for reference resources can be done at the library, at school, and sometimes at home.

The World Wide Web can be thought of as an illustrated version of the Internet. **Websites** or **web pages** contain pictures, sounds, and video files. These features make it fun to look for research references. They also make it possible to get a lot more information than a simple trip to your library or reading a book would yield. With some practice, you will be able to search the World Wide Web to find what you are looking for.

Search engines are the "tools" that you use to find information on the World Wide Web. Search engines provide a way for students to search for specific topics. Ask your teacher, media specialist, or parents to help you to connect to the Internet.

▶ DIRECTIONS

Once you are connected to the World Wide Web, use the search engine www.yahooligans.com, and type in the word *dolphin*. Then, click on the search button. Answer the questions.

1. How many category matches, or "hits," were listed? _____

2. How many site matches were listed? _____

3. Under which category do you find the most resources listed? _____

4. Are there any sites that have pictures of dolphins? _____

5. Are there any sites that have magazine articles listed? _____

Go on to the next page.

The Internet as a Reference Resource, p. 2

There is an enormous amount of information available on the World Wide Web. There are websites that have encyclopedias, dictionaries, magazine articles, and graphic resources. It is important to remember that much information available on the World Wide Web is not appropriate resource material. You may have to spend time deciding which is quality information and which is not.

D I R E C T I O N S

Using these different search engines, do a search for the subject *dolphin*. Then, answer the questions.

www.yahooligans.com
www.ajkids.com
www.altavista.com

1. Write the name of the search engine that gave you the best results. _____

2. Write the name of the search engine that gave the most results. _____

3. Which search engine was the hardest to use? _____

4. Which search engine gave you the most websites that had pictures of dolphins? _____

5. Did any search engine give you a website to go to that had sounds that dolphins make? _____

6. Which search engine gave the most magazine articles on dolphins? _____

7. Write the name of the search engine(s) that had websites with movies of dolphins. _____

   _____

8. Which search engine was the most fun to use? _____

   _____

9. If you were doing a report on how dolphins behave, which search engine would have helped

   you the most? _____

10. Pick a subject that interests you, and type the search word. Which search engine(s) did you use?

    Tell a little about what you found on your subject. _____

    _____

    _____

    _____

    _____

Name _____ Date _____

Narrowing the Search

Part of getting useful resources from the World Wide Web is learning how to narrow your search. **Browsing** the World Wide Web for a broad subject may give you so much information that it overwhelms you. Try to have the specific topic or interest so that you may find information quickly and effectively. Often, there are "**helpful tools**" known as **hints** or **tips** listed at each search engine site. These hints and tips will help you narrow your search. Try using the hints and tips if you find that you are receiving too many listings of websites in your initial search.

DIRECTIONS

Using the search engines listed, type the word *dolphin,* and do a search. When the particular search engine offers tips or hints, type the words *dolphin + behavior.* Then, answer the questions.

www.yahooligans.com
www.ajkids.com
www.altavista.com

1. Did you find more or fewer websites offered when you used the words

   dolphin + behavior? _____

2. Did any of the three search engines not change its listings when you used the words

   dolphin + behavior? _____

3. Are there any websites listed by any of the search engines that would give you information about dolphins and how they communicate? If so, write the addresses of the websites.

   _____

   _____

4. List four subjects relating to dolphin behavior.

   _____

   _____

   _____

   _____

5. List two website links where you found information for exercise 4.

   _____

   _____

Name _____   Date _____

Online Reference Resources

There are many websites available that will help you find the traditional reference resources. Many associations and organizations, such as the American Library Association, NASA, and the U.S. Library of Congress, have put their information online, so that it is easy to access. The media specialist at your school or library can help you with both online and conventional methods of resource gathering.

DIRECTIONS

Use the websites listed below to answer the questions.

Organization	Website
U.S. Library of Congress	http://lcweb.loc.gov/global/
The American Library Association	http://www.ala.org/ICONN/kidsconn.html
Librarians Web Search for Kids	http://sunsite.berkeley.edu/KidsClick!/
The WWW Virtual Library	http://vlib.org/Overview.html
The Internet Public Library Youth Division	http://www.ipl.org/youth/

1. Which website has an electronic Dewey Decimal Catalog? _____

2. Which websites have subjects listed alphabetically? _____

   _____

   _____

3. Which websites have subjects listed by categories? _____

   _____

   _____

4. Which is your favorite website? _____

5. Which website has a Story Hour section? _____

6. Which websites have fun activities for students to do? _____

   _____

7. Which websites do you think could help you the most on a research report? _____

   _____

8. Pick a subject that interests you. Use three different websites to find out more about the subject. List the three websites you used. Use your research to write a short description about the subject you chose. _____

   _____

   _____

   _____

Brainstorming

Brainstorming is a way to bring as many ideas to mind as you can. It is a particularly good way to get an idea for a paper if you have not been assigned a specific topic. You can brainstorm by yourself or with others. As you brainstorm, write down your ideas. When you think of ideas, it is not necessary to write them in sentence form.

DIRECTIONS

Read the topics below. Choose one topic, and circle it. Then, brainstorm about its advantages and disadvantages. Write down as many ideas as you can.

a. volunteering

b. eating healthy food

c. music

d. movies

e. good books

f. homework

_____

_____

_____

_____

_____

DIRECTIONS

Now, write a brief paragraph about the topic you chose in the exercise above that explains either the advantages or disadvantages of the topic.

_____

_____

_____

_____

_____

_____

_____

Name _____   Date _____

Fact and Opinion

In the body of the essay, your three developmental paragraphs may contain **opinions**. It is very important to back up opinions with **facts**. Facts can also be the supporting details for your topic sentences. Remember to keep facts and opinions separate from each other. If you separate the two, you will not confuse your audience, and you will achieve better coherence.

DIRECTIONS

Read the following dialogue. Write *fact* in front of the sentence if the speaker has expressed a fact. Write *opinion* if the speaker has expressed an opinion.

_____ **1.** "Quite a few people say they have seen the Loch Ness monster," said Justin.

_____ **2.** "That many people can't be wrong," said Matt.

_____ **3.** "Aw, they're all a bunch of nuts," said Tommy.

_____ **4.** "Yes," said Adam. "They should be ignored."

_____ **5.** "It's people like you who ought to be ignored," responded Matt.

_____ **6.** "Nobody has proved that there is a monster," Oliver pointed out.

_____ **7.** "Yes," Justin agreed. "A hundred and fifty years ago, scientists didn't believe the giant squid existed."

_____ **8.** "Probably most people wouldn't believe in elephants if scientists hadn't seen them," Clifton commented.

_____ **9.** "Loch Ness is deeper than other lakes in the area," said Timmy.

_____ **10.** "It has not been completely explored," added Joel.

DIRECTIONS

Take notes from the information listed above.

_____

_____

_____

_____

_____

_____

_____

Note Taking

Note taking is a useful way of recording information. A writer takes notes to remember important facts that he or she finds when preparing to write a report.

1. Note taking is an important step when writing a report.
2. You can find information for reports in encyclopedias, books, and magazines, and on the Internet.
3. Before you begin, organize your research questions.
4. Write information accurately and in your own words.
5. Take more notes than you need, so you won't have to go back to your sources a second time.
6. If you use a direct quotation, quote exactly. Enclose the quotation in quotation marks.

DIRECTIONS

Underline a topic below that interests you.

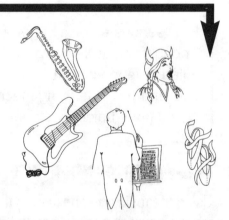

a favorite hobby   a favorite sport

the stars or planets   a favorite food

a historical figure   fashion or costumes

a species of animal   gardening

movies   airplanes

DIRECTIONS

Gather some sources of information about your topic. Write the name of the topic on the first line below. For example, if you have chosen "a favorite food," you might write the name of that particular food. Then, write notes about the topic on the remaining lines.

_____

_____

_____

_____

_____

_____

_____

Go on to the next page.

Note Taking, p. 2

How to Use Note Cards:

1. Use a single note card for each topic or question.
2. Write the topic or question at the top of the card.
3. Add the title, author, and page of the book you used.
4. Write important facts and details. Use key words and phrases.
5. Be sure your notes are accurate and reliable.
6. If you use a direct quotation, quote exactly. Enclose the quotation in quotation marks.

Example note card

Leonardo da Vinci's works in aeronautics
From <u>Pioneers of Flight</u> by Peter Buchard, page 12

First serious studies of aeronautics
Thought about "flapping" and "gliding"
Filled notebooks with sketches of birds' wings and
tails and possible flying machines
Notes not studied by others until nineteenth century

DIRECTIONS

Using the topic you chose from the examples on page 15, prepare note cards for that particular topic. Use extra paper if needed.

_____
_____
_____
_____
_____
_____
_____
_____

Topic and Audience

The **topic** of a story, article, or essay is the subject written about. The **audience** is the group of readers. Examples of readers are students, teachers, family members, neighbors, and readers of a newspaper.

▶ DIRECTIONS

Choose the most likely audience for each topic listed. Write the letter of the correct answer next to each topic.

a. first-graders   **c.** high-school students
b. the city council   **d.** parents

_____ **1.** Star Athlete Visits Students at Recreation Center

_____ **2.** Study Shows Connection between Time Spent Exercising and Student Progress in School

_____ **3.** Peter Rabbit Here for Hop and Jump Exercises

_____ **4.** Council Considers Tax Plans to Finance Recreation Center

_____ **5.** Tryouts for High-School Track Team on Friday

_____ **6.** Study Shows City Budget Shortfall Next Year

_____ **7.** Kelsey School Parents' Night Next Thursday

_____ **8.** Safety Officer to Visit Young Students Next Week

_____ **9.** State University Considers Raising Tuition

_____ **10.** Governor Approves Funds to Expand City Bus Service

▶ DIRECTIONS

Read the paragraph. Then, answer the questions.

On Tuesday evening, May 2, 2000, at 6:00, Hawkeye, the mascot of the Child Protection Foundation, will be at the park with his handler, Officer Roy Meyers. While Hawkeye, the long-eared hound, entertains the youngsters, Officer Meyers will discuss the topic "Keeping Your Children Safe." This unusual pair has traveled across the state to talk about topics such as accidents in the home, hazardous toys, and bike safety.

11. What is the topic of the paragraph? _____

12. Name two possible audiences for the paragraph. _____

13. Explain why each audience might be interested.

Audience 1: _____

Audience 2: _____

Go on to the next page.

Topic and Audience, p. 2

DIRECTIONS

Suppose that you chose the topic "watching TV." Underline the sentence that you would choose for the topic sentence.

1. Watching TV is one of the best ways to learn about things.

2. Watching TV is a waste of time.

3. The time children spend watching TV should be limited.

DIRECTIONS

Think about the topic sentence you chose in the first exercise. Then, underline the audience for whom you would like to write.

4. Your friends

5. Your family members

6. Readers of a newspaper

DIRECTIONS

Once you have picked your topic and audience, you are ready to collect information. Using a source or two, take notes to remember important facts that you find on this topic. Keep your audience in mind.

_____

_____

_____

_____

_____

_____

_____

_____

_____

_____

_____

Notes Based on an Interview

Many factual articles are based on information gathered in an **interview**. The writer asks someone questions about the subject he or she wants to cover and then uses the information to write an article.

DIRECTIONS

Read the notes from the interview. Then, read the paragraph that Anthony wrote, and answer the questions that follow.

Question 1: James, how do you feel about the proposed recreation center?

Answer: It is definitely needed. The park is too small for our growing city and needs massive repairs anyway. It will be good for the whole city to have a well-equipped recreation center.

Question 2: Your family has been involved in sports for many years. How do you feel about the modern approach to physical fitness for people of all ages?

Answer: Physical fitness is vital for everyone. That's why the new recreation center is so important. It will offer facilities and programs for everyone, regardless of age or current fitness levels.

Question 3: What will the recreation center include?

Answer: The center will house an indoor pool, a small ice rink, two gyms, meeting rooms, arts-and-crafts facilities, and locker rooms with showers. We also hope to include a weight-lifting room.

According to Mr. James DeLucia, park superintendent, the new recreation center will be a welcome addition to the city's facilities. The old park is now outdated and can no longer fill the needs of the people. Mr. DeLucia recommends that the park be the site of the new recreation center. Its facilities, which will include an indoor pool and two gyms, will fit everyone's needs, regardless of age or current fitness levels.

1. Does the author quote Mr. DeLucia exactly? _____

2. Write another question Anthony could have asked Mr. DeLucia. _____

_____

3. What other things will the recreation center include that were not mentioned in the article?

_____

_____

_____

Name _____ Date _____

Organizing and Taking Notes

Use this graphic organizer to help you take notes and keep your information organized.

Information Source

Topic _____

Title _____

Author _____

Name of magazine or research book (encyclopedia, atlas, or other source)

_____

Page or pages where information was found _____

Notes _____

_____

_____

_____

_____

_____

_____

Information Source

Topic _____

Title _____

Author _____

Name of magazine or research book (encyclopedia, atlas, or other source)

_____

Page or pages where information was found _____

Notes _____

_____

_____

_____

_____

_____

_____

Name _____   Date _____

Summarizing

When taking notes, you can use different methods for different sources of information. For note taking from a long passage such as a book, essay, or a lengthy article or report, you should use the **summarizing** method of note taking. When writing a summary, *do not* use whole sentences or many of the same phrases or the style of the original source. Be sure to include pertinent facts and supporting details in your notes.

DIRECTIONS

Read the following passage.

Safe Milk

Today we know the milk we buy is safe to drink. But this wasn't always so. In the 1800s, germs in milk spread many diseases. At last, a way to kill these germs was found. But it took years for this process to be accepted. And it might have taken longer if it hadn't been for Nathan Straus.

Nathan Straus and his brother, Isidor, were businessmen in New York City. They owned Macy's Department Store. Nathan Straus had read about Louis Pasteur. Pasteur had developed a way of heating milk to kill germs that cause disease. His method was called pasteurization. Straus became convinced that all milk should be pasteurized. His fight to convince others took twenty years.

In 1891, the first pasteurizer was put in a milk plant in the United States. But some fought this idea. Dairy farmers didn't want to buy the machine. Other people didn't think it was necessary. They thought keeping cows clean was enough to make milk safe.

In New York City, one child in ten died before the age of five. Straus was convinced that bad milk was one of the causes. He wanted to help. In 1893, he set up a stand and sold pasteurized milk in a poor neighborhood. He sold the milk for a low price. Many people bought milk there. The young children in the neighborhood became healthier. Few of them died. In the next few years, Straus set up twelve more stands.

In 1907, Straus and others wanted a law passed that would force milk producers to pasteurize milk. But those who sold milk were against the law. It was voted down. Straus kept fighting. He gave speeches, wrote letters, and spoke to the city leaders. Finally, pasteurization was accepted. By 1914, 95 percent of New York City's milk supply was pasteurized. The death rate of young children dropped almost at once. In 1923, Straus was given an award for his efforts to help the people of New York City.

Go on to the next page.

Summarizing, p. 2

DIRECTIONS

List the three most important ideas that you think were in the passage.

1. _____

2. _____

3. _____

DIRECTIONS

Take notes about the passage you just read using the *summarizing* method.

_____

_____

_____

_____

_____

_____

_____

_____

_____

_____

_____

_____

_____

_____

_____

_____

_____

_____

Paraphrasing

Another method of note taking is called **paraphrasing**. Paraphrasing is a way to reword, restate, or rephrase information you have gathered. This method is used for shorter passages or paragraphs. The same rules apply as for summarizing; do not use whole sentences or many of the same phrases or the style of the original source. Be sure to include pertinent facts and supporting details in your notes.

DIRECTIONS

Read the following passage. Then, take notes using the *paraphrasing* method.

"Four...three...two...one. And liftoff!" the announcer said. "Liftoff of the twenty-fifth space shuttle mission. And it has cleared the tower."

The children watching from the field broke into wild cheers, and they danced with joy. They saw the shuttle move up, up, up into the sky.

On board the *Challenger*, the crew members and others lay in place. The power of the blastoff pushed them deep into their seats. Commander Scobee talked on the radio with the control tower. At first, everything seemed normal. After 52 seconds, a controller told Scobee everything looked fine.

"*Challenger*, go with throttle up," the controller said. "Roger, go with throttle up," Scobee replied.

Scobee's words were spoken 70 seconds into the flight. Four seconds later, something horrible happened. Red, yellow, and orange flames shot out from the shuttle. The *Challenger* turned into a ball of fire, and it exploded into many pieces.

_____

_____

_____

_____

_____

_____

_____

_____

_____

_____

Go on to the next page.

Paraphrasing, p. 2

Read the following passages. Of the five passages below, circle the one from which you could best *paraphrase*.

1. The school children jumped up and down in the field. They were excited and couldn't wait for the big moment to arrive.

2. Back on Earth, no one could believe it. Some of the children in the field began crying. The controllers in the tower didn't know what to say as all around the world, people sat in shock.

3. People expressed their grief in many ways. Some kept their porch lights burning in memory of the shuttle crew. Others put up signs that said, *May They Rest In Peace*. President Reagan honored them in a speech, and Pope John Paul II said a special prayer. Everywhere people cried and prayed and hugged each other.

4. NASA did not launch another shuttle for more than two years. It worked to make sure that such a mistake would never happen again.

5. The *Challenger* disaster reminded everyone of the risks of space travel. Ronald McNair was one of the astronauts aboard the *Challenger*. Earlier he had said, "You can only become a winner if you are willing to walk over the edge." For their willingness to face the unknown, the crew of the *Challenger* will always be remembered.

Take notes using the *paraphrasing* method on the passage you selected.

_____

_____

_____

_____

_____

_____

_____

_____

_____

_____

_____

_____

Direct Quotations

The third method of note taking is using **direct quotations**. This method is used to take a quotation directly from a source. The information must be quoted exactly and enclosed in quotation marks. This should be the most concise form of note taking. Direct quotes should never make up more than 10% of your paper. Direct quotes are excellent as supporting details or even topic sentences.

DIRECTIONS

Read the passage. Choose quotations that you think are important or useful. Take notes using the proper method for *direct quotations*.

Solids, Liquids, and Gases

Everything around you is matter — the chair you are sitting on, the air around you. You are matter, too. All matter has some things in common. For instance, all matter takes up space. Matter is found on Earth in one of three states — solid, liquid, and gas. Matter in each of these states has different properties.

A *solid* has a definite shape and a definite volume. That is because its particles are very close together and are in a regular pattern. The particles move within the solid, but they are held together by an attraction. Heating a solid causes its particles to move more quickly, weakens the attraction between them, and produces melting.

A *liquid* does not have a definite shape. However, it does have a definite volume. The particles that make up a liquid move more quickly and freely than those in a solid. The attraction between them is not as strong as the attraction between the particles in a solid. The particles tumble over and around each other. A liquid flows and takes the shape of the container into which it is poured.

A *gas* does not have a definite shape or volume. The particles that make up a gas move quickly and freely. They don't have much attraction for one another. A gas spreads out to fill its container. The air around you is a gas.

Matter can change states. Solids can become liquids, and liquids can change to solids. Liquids can become gases, and gases can become liquids. How do all of these things happen? Heat. Heat is either added to or removed from matter to cause state changes.

Go on to the next page.

Direct Quotations, p. 2

Think about an ice cube. If you hold it in your hand, it gets warmer and begins to melt (becomes a liquid). However, if you put water in an ice cube tray and put it in the freezer, it freezes (becomes a solid). Climb out of a swimming pool on a hot day and watch what happens to your footprints as you walk across the cement. The liquid water evaporates to become water vapor in the air.

_____

_____

_____

_____

_____

_____

_____

_____

_____

_____

_____

_____

_____

_____

_____

_____

_____

_____

_____

Selecting Essential Information

During the note taking process, you must know what is **essential** or **relevant information** for your paper. You must read through your resources and determine what is necessary or unnecessary information. Only take notes on essential information.

■ D I R E C T I O N S ■

Read the topic sentence and the steps following it. Next to each step, write *E* if the information is essential to this how-to topic or *U* if the information is unnecessary. Tell why you think the step is unnecessary.

Topic Sentence: Diving safely requires preparing yourself and your equipment.

_____ **1.** Assemble your gear next to your air tank. _____

_____

_____ **2.** Fins that are too large will make you tire quickly. _____

_____

_____ **3.** Check the pressure gauge on your tank to be sure that your tank contains the necessary amount of air. _____

_____

_____ **4.** Next, check for leaks and tighten all valves. _____

_____

_____ **5.** A leaky valve will cause your air supply to run out more quickly than you expect.

_____

_____ **6.** Attach your tank to your stabilizing jacket before you suit up. _____

_____

_____ **7.** This eliminates having to attach your tank after your jacket is on. _____

_____

_____ **8.** To avoid cramped or pulled muscles in the water, perform mild stretching exercises before suiting up. _____

_____

_____ **9.** Hold your mask firmly with one hand and secure your regulator in your mouth with the other as you enter the water. _____

_____

Using Examples

To write a good paper, you must give enough information by choosing **effective** examples and the **right number** of examples.

DIRECTIONS

Read the following paragraphs. Label each paragraph as having the *right number* of examples, *too many*, or *too few*. If the paragraph has too few examples, write the examples you would add. If the paragraph has too many, write the examples that are not effective and should be crossed out.

1.   Wayne was a forgetful person. He was always leaving books on buses and benches. He often forgot to take his homework assignment home. When he did remember, he forgot to bring his completed assignment back to school. On those few occasions when he did bring a completed assignment back to school, Wayne usually forgot to turn it in.

_____

_____

_____

2.   That day everything went wrong for me. My breakfast was burned. My mother refused to buy me a horse. My hair would not curl right. I had to iron my shirt. The dog chewed up my homework. I studied the wrong pages for my test. Joan won the spelling bee, and I only came in second. Worst of all, Wayne was assigned as my partner for the oral science report.

_____

_____

_____

3.   Working with Wayne, however, turned out better than I thought. He came up with some good ideas for our report.

_____

_____

_____

_____

_____

Practice, Practice, Practice

When you have picked your topic and collected your resources, you are ready to take notes. It is up to you to decide which of the three methods, summarizing, paraphrasing, or direct quotations, is best suited for the reference material you have collected.

DIRECTIONS

Read the following passage. Decide which method is most appropriate for each passage, *summarizing, paraphrasing,* or *direct quotations*. List the method. Then, take notes on the passage using that method.

Water on the Earth

Every day we take many things for granted. One thing we take for granted is water. No plant or animal could live without water. It is needed for drinking, cleaning, and keeping us cool. Our bodies are about two thirds water. We need about a quart of water a day to replace the water we lose naturally. All the food we eat and the things we use every day required much water in their making.

Americans use a half trillion gallons of water a day. Each person in the United States uses about 90 gallons of water a day for cleaning and gardening. Two more gallons per person are used for drinking and cooking. Factories use lots of water to make goods. It takes 60,000 gallons of water to make one ton of steel. Farmers use 115 gallons of water to grow the wheat for one loaf of bread, and 4,000 gallons are needed to get one pound of beef. As you can see, water is very important to us all. We must always be sure to take care of the water we have.

Best Method: _____

_____

_____

_____

_____

_____

_____

_____

_____

_____

Go on to the next page.

Practice, Practice, Practice, p. 2

DIRECTIONS

Read the following passages. Take notes on these passages on page 31 using each of the three methods. Use additional paper if needed.

Water

Water is our most precious resource. Water covers about 70 percent of the Earth's surface. Without water, life could not exist. Our bodies are about 65 percent water. We use water in many ways. Water can be a solid, a liquid, and a gas. It can change from its solid state (ice) to its liquid state (water) to its gaseous state (water vapor) and back again.

Water in its solid state is good for cooling and preserving things, and for fun and recreation. Water as a liquid is very important, too. We use liquid water for drinking, for cooking, for cleaning, for swimming, and for watering plants.

Water as a gas is perhaps its most interesting form. Water as a gas is called water vapor. The amount of water vapor in the air is called humidity. Different air masses have different levels of humidity. Air, depending on its temperature, can hold only so much humidity. When too much humidity is in the air, some of it is released in the form of precipitation. Kinds of precipitation are rain, snow, sleet, hail, dew, frost, and fog.

The Water Cycle

Water often changes from its liquid form to its gaseous form and back to its liquid form in a process called the water cycle. The three main steps in the water cycle are evaporation, condensation, and precipitation. Evaporation is necessary to get the liquid water into its gaseous form of water vapor in the air. Condensation is needed to turn the vapor back to a liquid in the clouds. And precipitation returns the liquid water to the Earth.

Evaporation occurs as liquid water is heated and changed into water vapor. The water vapor is then carried up into the sky by rising air. Condensation takes place as the rising water vapor cools and is changed into liquid water, forming clouds. Precipitation happens as water droplets grow heavy and fall to the Earth as rain, snow, or some other type of precipitation.

Go on to the next page.

Practice, Practice, Practice, p. 3

The Oceans

The oceans cover about two thirds of the Earth's surface. The great majority of Earth's water is in the oceans, and most of this is salt water. The oceans can be several miles deep, but most of the life in the oceans exists in the top 200 meters of water.

Over nine tenths of the Earth's water is salty. Salt is a natural resource that is dissolved in ocean water. Salt water is not good for drinking. But objects do float more easily in salt water than in fresh water. Salt water also freezes more slowly than fresh water. This is one reason the oceans do not freeze in very cold climates.

The ocean floor is not a flat, wide plain. Instead, the ocean floor contains many of the same landform features found on the continents. The ocean floor does have plains, but it also has slopes, hills, mountains, valleys, and volcanoes. The oceans contain mid-ocean ridges, which are long chains of mountains that run along the ocean floor.

Measuring the depths of the oceans is not an easy task. Now scientists use a method called sonar. In this method, sound waves are aimed at the ocean floor. Based on their rate of travel, the sound waves can be timed. These times can then be used to calculate the depth of the ocean floor.

As the depth of the ocean water increases, its pressure also increases. As a result, deep-sea divers and explorers need to use special equipment and to observe certain procedures when they make their dives. One procedure is called decompression. In this procedure, divers must rise back to the surface slowly, or bubbles of nitrogen gas can occur in their blood, causing a painful condition called "the bends."

Summarizing: _____

_____

_____

_____

_____

_____

Paraphrasing: _____

_____

Direct Quotation: _____

_____

Introduction to Outlines

Now that you have collected your resources and taken notes from them, you can make an **outline** for your paper. An outline is used to organize main ideas and important details that will be used in the writing of your paper. An outline classifies the general subject into topics and subtopics. The general subject is introduced in the thesis statement. An outline is done in a narrative sequence, or the order in which you will present your material.

DIRECTIONS

Look at the example triangles. Notice how the first line contains a very general topic and then tapers down, narrowing the subject into more specific subtopics. Write in possible topics and subtopics below the general subject in the remaining triangles.

Example:

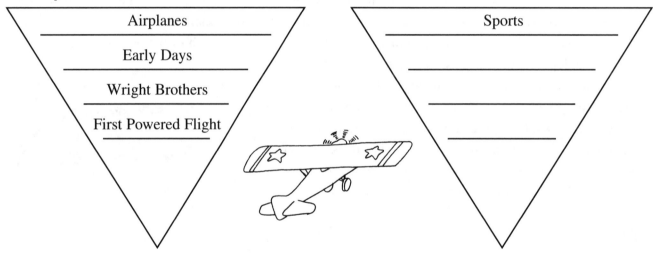

Airplanes

Early Days

Wright Brothers

First Powered Flight

Sports

Cuba

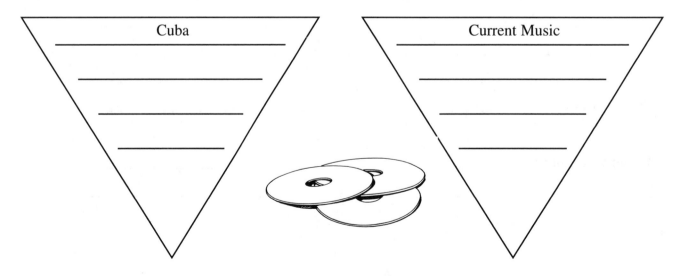

Current Music

Name _____   Date _____

Outlining a Plan

An **outline** is a plan to help organize writing. An outline lists the main ideas of a topic. An outline starts with a **statement** that tells the topic of the writing. The statement is followed by **main headings** and **subheadings** that tell what goes into each part. Main headings start with a Roman numeral followed by a period. They name the main ideas of a topic. Subheadings start with a capital letter followed by a period. They tell the details that support each main idea. Main headings and subheadings are written in phrases, or incomplete sentences. Each phrase begins with a capital letter.

Statement: First Aid for Burns

(Main heading)   I.   Keeping the wound clean
(Subheadings)   A. Applying thick, clean dressing
               B. Avoiding sprays or oils

(Main heading)   II.   Easing pain
(Subheadings)   A. Applying ice packs
               B. Putting injured area in ice water

DIRECTIONS

Look at the outline below. Write the Roman numerals and capital letters before each phrase to show the correct way to make an outline. Then, write *main heading* or *subheading* to tell what the phrases are. The first one is done for you.

Statement: Rabbits

I.   Appearance of rabbits _____ main heading _____

_____   Long ears _____

_____   Sharp teeth _____

_____   Strong hind legs _____

_____   Habits of rabbits _____

_____   Feed at night _____

_____   Kick and bite _____

_____   Kinds of rabbits _____

_____   Jackrabbit _____

_____   Cottontail _____

Go on to the next page.

Outlining a Plan, p. 2

A writer uses an **outline** to organize the information he or she has gathered to write a report. An outline lists the main ideas and the details of a topic.

How to Make an Outline:
1. Write a statement that tells the topic of the writing.
2. Write each main idea as a main heading. Use a Roman numeral and a period.
3. Write each detail as a subheading. Indent and use a capital letter followed by a period.
4. Begin the first word in each line with a capital letter.
5. Do not write a *I* without a *II* or an *A* without a *B*.
6. Plan one paragraph for each main topic in your outline.
7. Sometimes, order is important when writing the subheadings. If a process is described, write the details in the order the steps occur.

DIRECTIONS

Look at the outline below. Write a statement. Then, write each detail from the box under the correct main heading.

Root	Air	Leaf
Water	Sunlight	Stem

Statement: _____

I. Plant parts

    A. _____

    B. _____

    C. _____

II. Things plants need to grow

    A. _____

    B. _____

    C. _____

Outlining

The purpose and structure of an outline are to organize your material. There is a very specific way to do this, and it is a standard outline construction.

How to Write an Outline:

1. Use a Roman numeral for each main idea and a capital letter for each detail that supports the main idea.
2. Capitalize the first letter of every topic and detail.
3. Keep outline entries short and specific.
4. Do not write a *I* without a *II* or an *A* without a *B*.
5. Write entries that are similar in wording.

Example Outline

A Short History of Flight

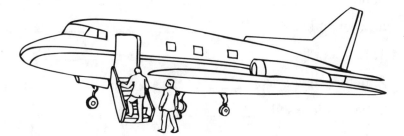

   I. Introduction—stories of flight
  II. Early days of flight
     A. Leonard da Vinci
     B. Montgolfier brothers
 III. Development of flight
     A. Otto Lilienthal
     B. Wright brothers
 IV. Flight today
     A. Yuri Gagarin
     B. Neil Armstrong and Edwin Aldrin
     C. John Young and Robert Crippen
  V. Conclusion—future of flight

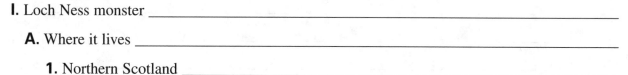

DIRECTIONS

Write *main topic*, *subtopic*, or *detail* to identify each item in this part of an outline.

  I. Loch Ness monster _____

   A. Where it lives _____

    1. Northern Scotland _____

    2. Deep, narrow lake _____

   B. What it looks like _____

    1. Small head _____

    2. Long, thin neck _____

    3. Body about 90 feet long _____

Go on to the next page.

Name _____   Date _____

Outlining, p. 2

How to Write an Outline:
1. Use a Roman numeral for each main idea and a capital letter for each detail that supports the main idea.
2. Capitalize the first letter of every topic and detail.
3. Keep outline entries short and specific.
4. Do not write a *I* without a *II* or an *A* without a *B*.
5. Write entries that are similar in wording.

DIRECTIONS

The lines in this part of the outline are in the *correct order*. Find the error or errors in each line, and write the line correctly. Remember to indent the lines properly.

II. the Yeti _____

a. where it lives _____

1. In Asia _____

2. in the Himalayas _____

b. what it looks like _____

1. large ape or man _____

2. covered with hair _____

DIRECTIONS

Choose a topic that interests you. Then, write an outline for that topic. Write the topic, the main idea, and the supporting details. Use the structure shown below. Use another piece of paper if necessary.

Topic: _____

I. _____

   A. _____

   B. _____

II. _____

   A. _____

   B. _____

III. _____

   A. _____

   B. _____

Thesis Statements and Outlines

A **thesis statement** defines the topic for the whole essay. The thesis statement indicates the reason or intent for the essay in relation to your topic. Your outline should support your thesis statement.

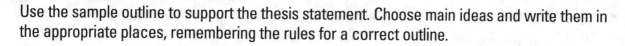

D I R E C T I O N S

Use the sample outline to support the thesis statement. Choose main ideas and write them in the appropriate places, remembering the rules for a correct outline.

Thesis Statement: Dolphins are one of the smartest creatures on the planet.

I. _____

     (Main Heading)

  A. _____

     (Subheading)

  B. _____

     (Subheading)

  C. _____

     (Subheading)

II. _____

     (Main Heading)

  A. _____

     (Subheading)

  B. _____

     (Subheading)

  C. _____

     (Subheading)

III. _____

     (Main Heading)

  A. _____

     (Subheading)

  B. _____

     (Subheading)

  C. _____

     (Subheading)

Supporting Details and Outlines

The idea expressed in a topic sentence or main idea can be developed with sentences containing **supporting details**. Details can include facts, examples, and reasons. The supporting details should be included in an outline.

DIRECTIONS

Use the sample outline to support the thesis statement. Choose main ideas and supporting details. Then, write them in the appropriate places, remembering the rules for a correct outline.

Thesis Statement: Water is one of our most important natural resources.

I. _____
   (Main Heading)

   A. _____
      (Subheading)

   B. _____
      (Subheading)

   C. _____
      (Subheading)

II. _____
   (Main Heading)

   A. _____
      (Subheading)

   B. _____
      (Subheading)

   C. _____
      (Subheading)

III. _____
   (Main Heading)

   A. _____
      (Subheading)

   B. _____
      (Subheading)

   C. _____
      (Subheading)

Footnotes and Appendix

There are two parts of a book that might be new to you, **footnotes** and the **appendix**. Footnotes appear in two different ways according to the date of the book or publication you are using. Older reference resources will show footnotes at the bottom of the page. A small number next to a word or phrase in the material tells you to look at the bottom of the page for a matching number. There, you will be given additional information. It might be an explanation of the meaning of special terms, or the sources of facts, ideas, or quotations. New material may contain the same small number in the material, but the information is at the end of the essay instead of the bottom of the page.

The appendix is a section at the end of the book in which an author gives additional information to help the reader understand the material in the book. The appendix is usually found in a nonfiction book and might contain charts, maps, graphs, tables, or other material.

To Use Footnotes and the Appendix:
1. Read the material carefully.
2. Notice if footnotes are used, and, if so, take advantage of the helpful information.
3. Check to see if there is an appendix in the back of the book that might have helpful information.

DIRECTIONS

Write *footnote* or *appendix* next to each description to tell where it might be found.

_____ **1.** bottom of page

_____ **2.** graph or map

_____ **3.** end of book

_____ **4.** gives a meaning

_____ **5.** gives a source

_____ **6.** table or chart

Go on to the next page.

Footnotes and Appendix, p. 2

To Use Footnotes and the Appendix:
1. Read the material carefully.
2. Notice if footnotes are used, and, if so, take advantage of the helpful information.
3. Check to see if there is an appendix in the back of the book that might have helpful information.

DIRECTIONS

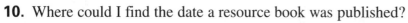

Circle the letter by of the choice that best answers the question.

7. Where could I find the name of the author of the book?
   A. footnote
   B. appendix
   C. elsewhere

8. Where could I find a list of chess clubs in a book about championship chess?
   A. footnote
   B. appendix
   C. elsewhere

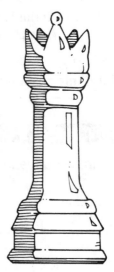

9. Where could I find the source of a quotation on a page?
   A. footnote
   B. appendix
   C. elsewhere

10. Where could I find the date a resource book was published?
    A. footnote
    B. appendix
    C. elsewhere

11. Where could I find a map of the sites of Civil War memorials in a book about the Civil War?
    A. footnote
    B. appendix
    C. elsewhere

Name _____ Date _____

Documenting Your Sources

When you decide to use a source, make sure you gather all the publication data that you will need to document the source. In fact, you should gather this data before you take any notes. If you use the source material without providing citation and documentation, you are technically guilty of plagiarism. Be sure, also, if you copy the source material word for word, that you enclose the material in quotation marks.

There are many ways to document your information in your paper. You always put the identifying information in parentheses following the borrowed information.

DIRECTIONS

Gather some resource materials, including different types of books, magazine articles, and Internet sources. Look for the different types of documentation and citation provided by each source. Write the name of the source on one line. Then, below that, copy the documentation and citation style exactly. Using various sources, you should be able to see different styles of documentation.

1. Source: _____

   Documentation: _____

   _____

2. Source: _____

   Documentation: _____

   _____

3. Source: _____

   Documentation: _____

   _____

4. Source: _____

   Documentation: _____

   _____

Go on to the next page.

Documenting Your Sources, p. 2

In the exercise on page 41, you probably noted many different types of documentation and citation. The source and the date the source was published would have an effect on this. Following is the newer method used, including some of the rules.

Rule 1: When you introduce material without using the author's name, give the author's last name and page number(s) within parentheses.
Example: (Smith 91)

Rule 2: When you use the author's name in your writing to introduce material you used, give only the page number(s) within parentheses.
Example: (91)

Rule 3: If you use a source with more than one author and you do not mention them in your paper, give all of their last names and page number(s) in the parentheses.
Example: (Smith and Jones 33)

DIRECTIONS

Using the same sources you used in the exercise on page 41, copy the documentation and citation. Then, below that, write the rule number from above or *not found* if it is a different style.

1. Documentation: _____

_____

Rule Number: _____

2. Documentation: _____

_____

Rule Number: _____

3. Documentation: _____

_____

Rule Number: _____

4. Documentation: _____

_____

Rule Number: _____

Name _____   Date _____

Writing a Bibliography

In a **bibliography**, a writer lists the sources used to gather information for a research report. The bibliography gives credit to the author of the material. The bibliography is sometimes called **Works Cited**. Each part of the reference made to a source is a bibliographic "sentence" that ends with a period.

How to Write a Bibliography:

1. List the sources in alphabetical order by the author's last name.
2. Write the title of the source after the author's name. Then, list the publisher and the date of publication.
3. If the author's name is not listed, use the first important word of the title in alphabetical order.

Books
Bishop, Richard W. From Kite to Kitty Hawk. New York: Thomas Y. Crowell Company, 1978.
Davidson, Jesse. Famous Firsts in Aviation. New York: G.P. Putnam's Sons, 1974.
Article in Encyclopedia
Fraser, Robert C. "Aviation." World Book Encyclopedia, vol. 1, pp. 955–964. Chicago: World Book, Inc., 1986.
Magazine Article
"Superfast Plane Scheduled for 1990s." Current Events, May 2, 1986, p. 3.

DIRECTIONS

Use the bibliography above to answer these questions.

1. What are three kinds of sources the writer used? _____

_____

2. Where and when was *Famous Firsts in Aviation* published? _____

_____

3. Which source does not give the name of the author? _____

_____

4. What is the title of the encyclopedia article by Robert C. Fraser? _____

_____

Go on to the next page.

Writing a Bibliography, p. 2

How to Write a Bibliography:
1. List the sources in alphabetical order by the author's last name.
2. Write the title of the source after the author's name. Then, list the publisher and the date of publication.
3. If the author's name is not listed, use the first important word of the title in alphabetical order.

DIRECTIONS

Find the error or errors in each bibliography entry. Write the entry correctly.

1. Zimnik, Reiner, <u>The Bear on the Motorcycle</u>, New York—Atheneum, 1963

_____

_____

2. "Pioneer Country Pies," <u>Sunset: The Magazine of Western Living</u>, Nov. 1988 (p.104)

_____

_____

3. <u>The Complete Home Guide to all the Vitamins</u> by Ruth Adams. New York: Larchmont Books. 1972

_____

_____

DIRECTIONS

Write the following items as bibliography entries.

4. A book by Henry James titled <u>The Awkward Age</u>, published in New York by Anchor Books in 1958

_____

_____

5. A book called <u>Birds of North America</u>, written by Chandler Robbins and published by Western Publishing Company of Racine, Wisconsin, in 1986

_____

_____

Practice, Practice

DIRECTIONS

Read the passage below. Construct an outline for it. Write the thesis statement, main ideas, and supporting details.

Stormy Weather

One of the most common examples of foul weather is the thunderstorm. Approaching thunderstorms are often accompanied by towering cumulus clouds called thunderheads. These billowy clouds have flat tops and dark bottoms. Thunderheads are formed when warm, moist air rises. As the rising air begins to cool, water vapor in the air condenses, and cumulus clouds form. The hot ground causes the heated air to rise faster and higher. The cumulus clouds grow larger and taller, often reaching ten miles or more into the air. As the clouds grow in size, they become more likely to produce rain.

Thunderheads also produce two well-known features of stormy weather—lightning and thunder. Lightning is an electrical spark caused by friction inside the thunderhead. As the clouds grow, raindrops scrape against each other, and friction is produced. This friction builds up an electrical charge, just as you do when you scrape your feet across a carpet. Most of the electric charges in the lower part of the cloud are negative. These negative charges emit a spark that jumps toward a positive charge on the charge. This spark is what we call lightning.

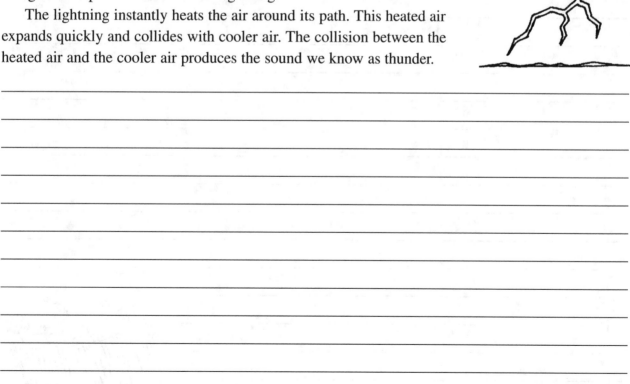

The lightning instantly heats the air around its path. This heated air expands quickly and collides with cooler air. The collision between the heated air and the cooler air produces the sound we know as thunder.

_____
_____
_____
_____
_____
_____
_____
_____
_____
_____
_____
_____
_____

Go on to the next page.

Practice, Practice, p. 2

DIRECTIONS

Read the passage again. Then, take notes using the best method for this kind of passage.

_____
_____
_____
_____
_____
_____
_____
_____
_____
_____

_____
_____
_____
_____
_____
_____
_____
_____
_____
_____
_____
_____
_____
_____
_____
_____

Posttest

DIRECTIONS

Circle the letter by the part of the book in which you would find the information.

1. The name of the author
  A. title page
  B. copyright page
  C. table of contents
  D. index

2. The page at the back of the book that lists where certain information can be found
  A. title page
  B. copyright page
  C. table of contents
  D. index

3. The date the book was published
  A. title page
  B. copyright page
  C. table of contents
  D. index

4. How many units are in the book
  A. title page
  B. copyright page
  C. table of contents
  D. index

DIRECTIONS

Circle the correct answer to each question.

5. Where would you find the publisher of a book?

  A. table of contents   **B.** index   **C.** copyright page

6. Where would you find chapter titles?

  A. table of contents   **B.** index   **C.** title page

DIRECTIONS

Tell which kind of catalog card you would refer to to find each book. Circle (A) for author card, (B) for subject card, or (C) for title card.

7. A book about volcanoes in Hawaii   **A.**   **B.**   **C.**

8. *To Kill a Mockingbird*   **A.**   **B.**   **C.**

9. A book of short stories by O. Henry   **A.**   **B.**   **C.**

10. A book about Grandma Moses   **A.**   **B.**   **C.**

11. A book of poems by Carl Sandburg   **A.**   **B.**   **C.**

12. *The Story of Martin Luther King*   **A.**   **B.**   **C.**

Go on to the next page.

Posttest, p. 2

DIRECTIONS

Read the following paragraph. Use the information to complete the section of an outline below.

The red-headed woodpecker lives in areas from Florida to the Canadian border, and ranges as far west as North Dakota. It prefers deciduous woods. Like other woodpeckers, it has a long, sharp bill for digging into trees trunks and a stiff tail. Its boring makes a drumming noise on tree limbs. It has a completely red head and a white patch on its wing that distinguishes it from other woodpeckers. Its call is a raucous *kwrrk*.

13.

   I. Red-headed woodpecker

      A. Where it can be found

         1. _____

         2. _____

      B. Characteristics _____

         1. _____

         2. _____

         3. _____

DIRECTIONS

Write bibliography entries for the following information.

14. A book called *Birds of North America*, written by Chandler Robbins and published by Western Publishing Company of Racine, Wisconsin, in 1986

_____

_____

15. An encyclopedia entry on woodpeckers in *The Natural Sciences Encyclopedia* (with no author listed) published by Crown Publishers of London in 1988

_____

_____